The Circulatory System

Why Does My Heart Beat?

Sue Barraclough

Heinemann Library
Chicago, Illinois

Customer Service   888-454-2279

Photo research by Hannah Taylor and Maria Joannou
Designed by Debbie Oatley and Steve Mead
Printed and bound in China by South China Printing Company

ISBN 978-1-4329-0869-0

12 11 10 09 08
10 9 8 7 6 5 4 3 2 1

Library of Congress Cataloging-in-Publication Data

Barraclough, Sue.
  The circulatory system : why does my heart beat? / Sue Barraclough.
    p. cm. – (Body systems)
  Includes bibliographical references and index.
  ISBN 978-1-4329-0869-0 (hc) – ISBN 978-1-4329-0875-1 (pb) 1. Blood–Circulation–Juvenile literature. 2. Cardiovascular system–Juvenile literature. I. Title.
  QP103.B36 2008
  612.1'1–dc22
                              2008001156

Acknowledgements
The publishers would like to thank the following for permission to reproduce photographs: ©Alamy p.**14** (Elvele Images); ©Corbis pp.**7** (Brand X, Triolo Productions, Burke), **4** (Chase Jarvis), **24** (Fabio Cardoso), **16** (John Lund, Tiffany Schoepp, Blend Images), **18** (Ralf Schultheiss, Zefa), **9** (Roy McMahon), **26** (Roy Morsch); ©Getty Images pp.**12**, **8** (Stone); ©Rex Features p.**6** (Image Source); ©Science Photo Library pp.**5** (Alfred Pasieka), **10**, **20**, **22** (Susumu Nishinaga)

Cover photograph of a boy riding a bicycle reproduced with permission of ©Getty Images (DK Stock).

Contents

Some words are shown in bold, **like this**. You can find out what they mean by looking in the glossary.

What Is My Heart?

Your **heart** is a muscle inside your chest. Your heart moves blood around your body. Blood helps your body to keep warm and to move.

Your heart beats faster when you move. It slows down when you are resting or sleeping.

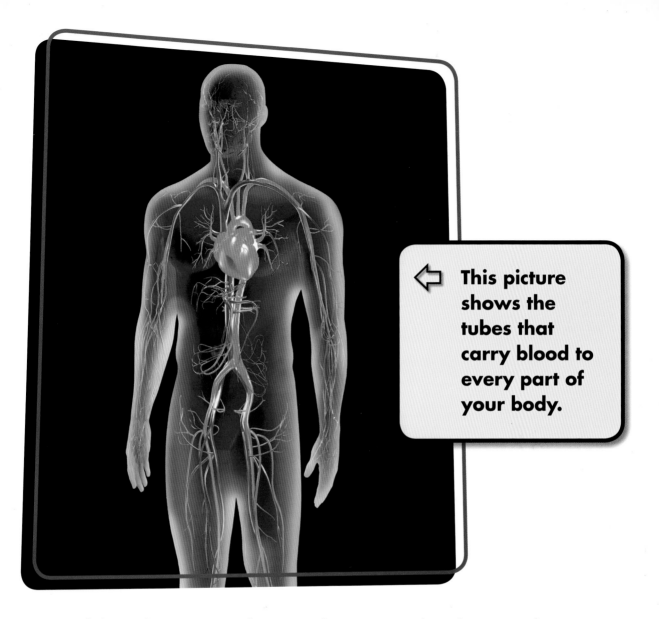

This picture shows the tubes that carry blood to every part of your body.

Your blood carries things that your body needs to keep it working. Your heart is linked to tubes called **blood vessels**. These tubes take blood to every part of your body.

What Is My Circulatory System?

Circulation means moving things around. The circulatory system is made of different parts that move blood around your body. There are parts you can see such as **blood vessels**. Your blood moves through them under your skin.

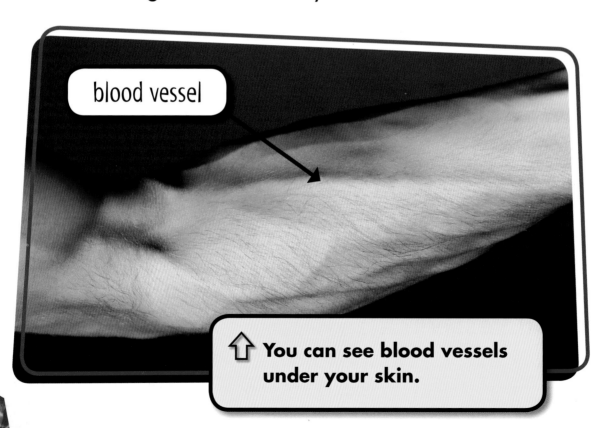

blood vessel

⬆ **You can see blood vessels under your skin.**

You can feel your heart beating inside your body. ⬆

There are parts inside your body that you cannot see, such as your **heart**. These and other parts work together to move blood around your body.

What Is Blood?

⬆ **Different parts of your body need oxygen and nutrients to make them work.**

Blood is a liquid that is pumped around your body. Its main job is to carry **oxygen** and **nutrients** to your body parts. It also takes away **waste** that your body does not need.

Oxygen is a gas that your body uses to get **energy** from your food. Nutrients are the useful parts of food. **Glucose** is the nutrient that is broken down with oxygen to give you energy.

⇧ **All kinds of food can be broken down to give you energy.**

What Are Blood Cells?

Your blood is made of different types of **cells** carried in a liquid called **plasma**. Cells are tiny living parts that fit together to make your body. Each type of blood cell has a different job to do.

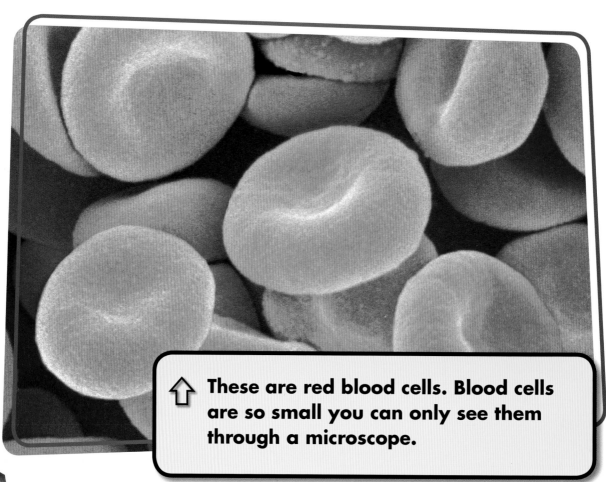

⬆ **These are red blood cells. Blood cells are so small you can only see them through a microscope.**

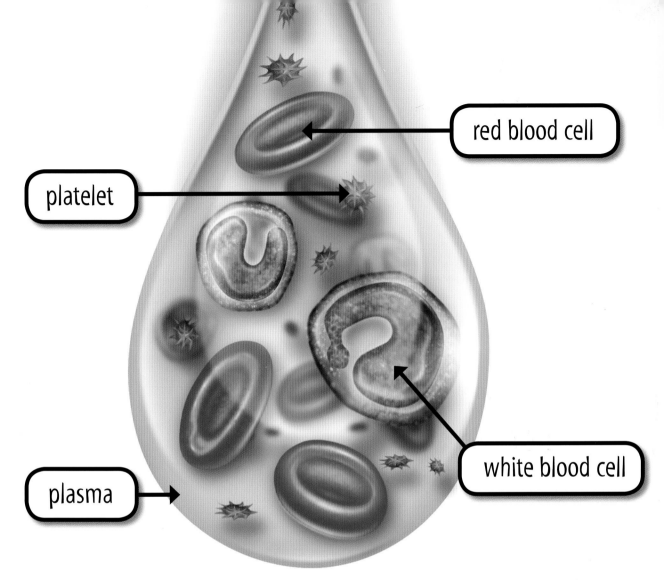

red blood cell

platelet

white blood cell

plasma

There are three types of blood cells. Red blood cells carry **oxygen**. White blood cells protect you from germs and illness. **Platelets** make your blood **clot**. If you cut yourself they stop you from bleeding too much.

What Does My Heart Do?

The **heart** is a powerful pump that works non-stop to move blood around your body. Your heart is in the middle of your chest. It sits between your **lungs**.

⬇ **You can hear your heart beating.**

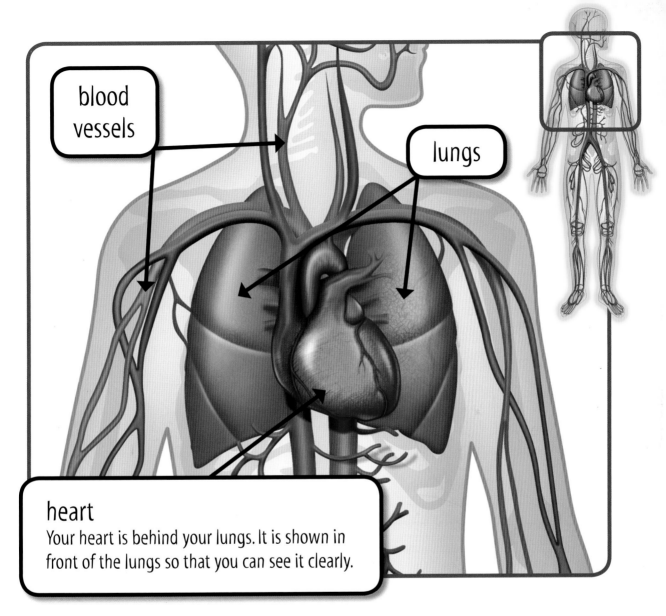

blood
vessels

lungs

heart
Your heart is behind your lungs. It is shown in
front of the lungs so that you can see it clearly.

The heart pulls in blood and pumps it out again.
Your heart has tubes called **blood vessels** linked
to it. The blood vessels carry blood in and out of
the heart.

How Does My Heart Work?

When you run you breathe faster and your heart pumps faster.

Your **heart** pumps blood out to the **lungs** to collect **oxygen**. The lungs fill the blood with oxygen. Then the blood is moved back into the heart.

The heart pumps the blood into an **artery**. It is pushed around the body in the **blood vessels**.

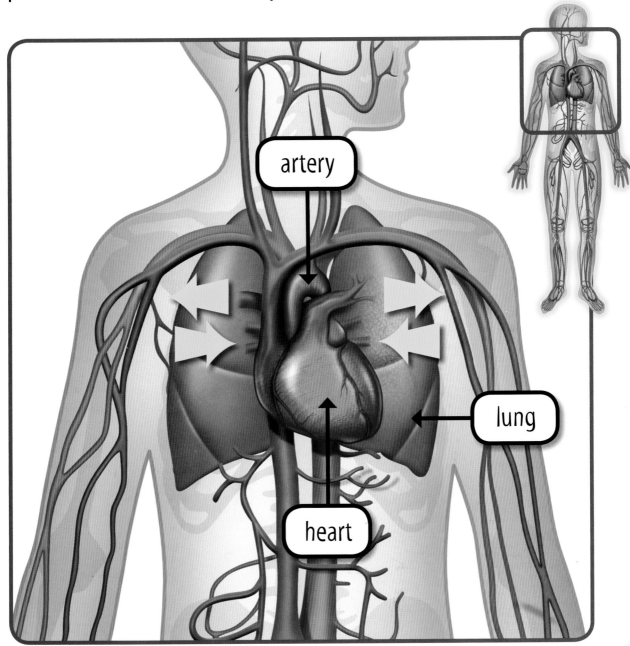

artery

lung

heart

What Are Blood Vessels?

Blood vessels are tubes that are joined to the **heart**. They take blood to every part of your body. There are three types of blood vessels. They are **arteries**, **veins**, and **capillaries**.

By taking your blood pressure, doctors can find out about how the blood is moving through your arteries.

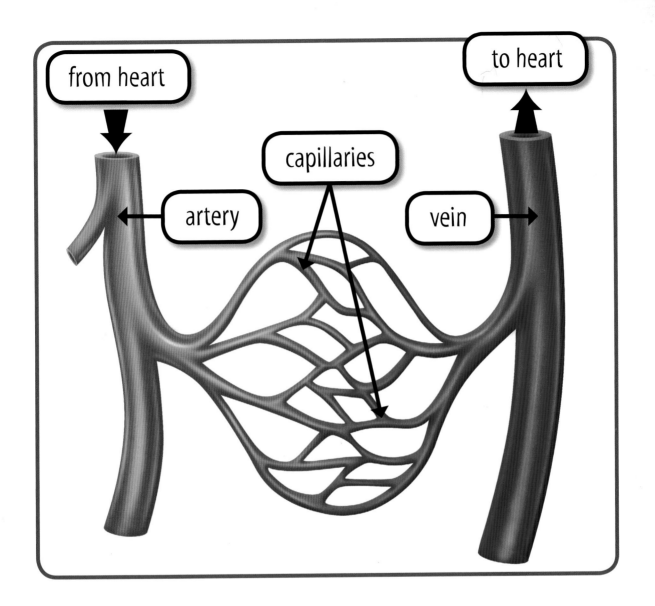

from heart

to heart

capillaries

artery

vein

Each type of blood vessel does a different job. Arteries carry blood away from the heart. Veins carry blood back to the heart. Tiny blood vessels called capillaries link the arteries and veins.

What Do My Arteries Do?

Arteries are the biggest and strongest **blood vessels**. They are stretchy tubes with thick walls. They need to be strong because they carry the blood pumped out of the **heart**.

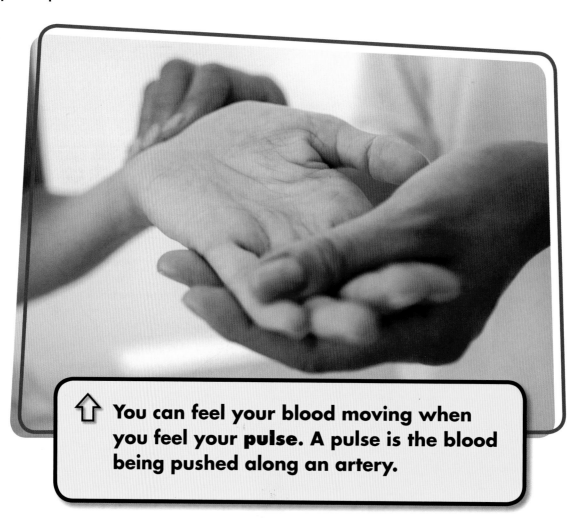

⇧ **You can feel your blood moving when you feel your pulse. A pulse is the blood being pushed along an artery.**

The blood is pumped out of the heart into a big artery. As the blood travels away from the heart the arteries get smaller and smaller.

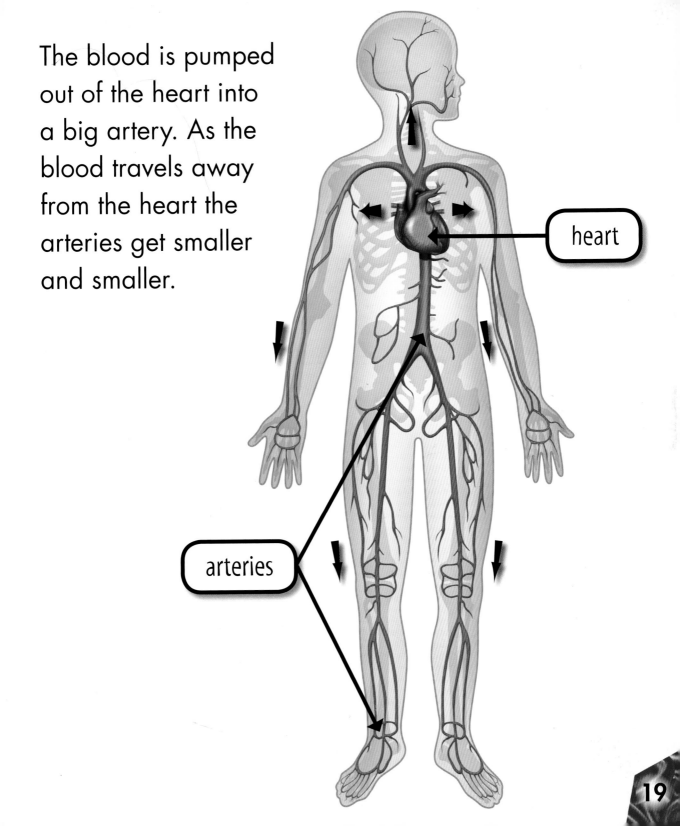

heart

arteries

What Do My Capillaries Do?

Capillaries carry blood from your **arteries**. Capillaries have thin walls. This means **oxygen** and **nutrients** can pass into **cells** in the body. Your cells use oxygen and nutrients to produce **energy**.

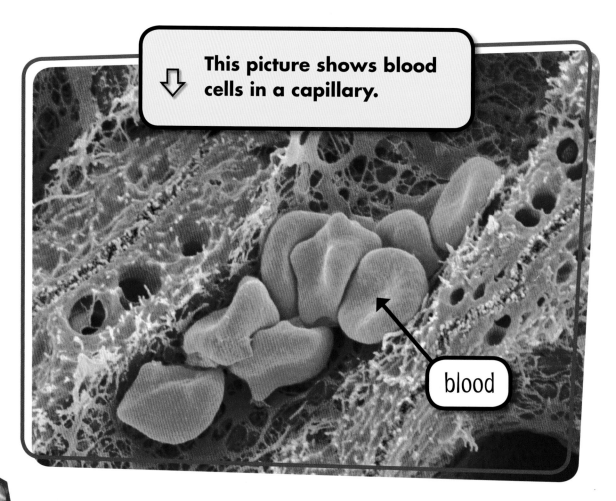

This picture shows blood cells in a capillary.

blood

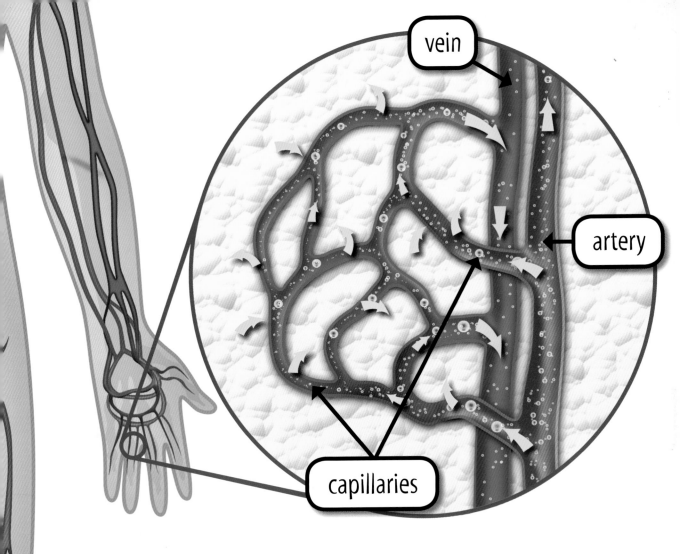

vein

artery

capillaries

When the cells use oxygen they make a **waste** gas called **carbon dioxide**. Carbon dioxide passes back into the blood in the capillaries. The blood then travels into your **veins**.

What Do My Veins Do?

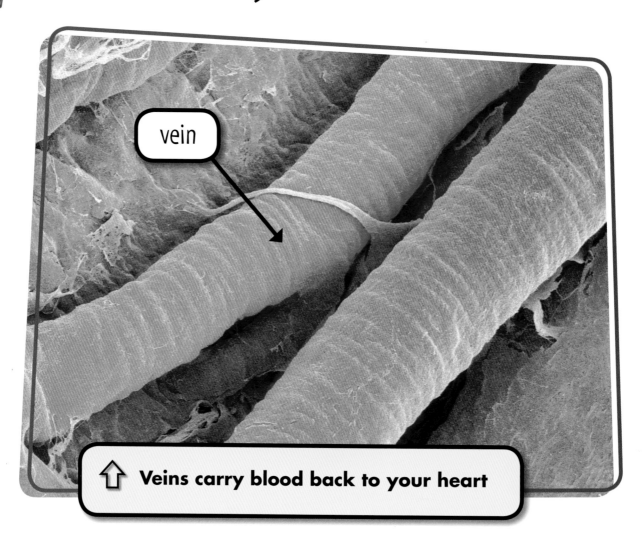

vein

⇧ **Veins carry blood back to your heart**

The blood in your **veins** carries **carbon dioxide**. This is a gas your body does not need. Your body needs to get rid of the carbon dioxide.

The blood travels through your veins to get back to your **heart**. As the blood travels towards the heart the veins get bigger and wider.

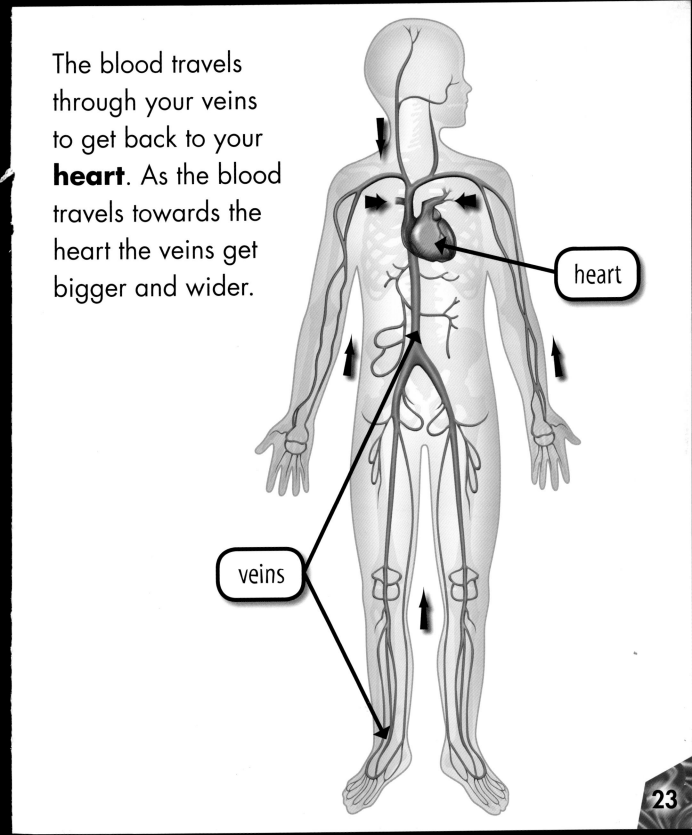

heart

veins

Why Is Blood Moved Back To My Heart?

Blood is taken back to your **heart** carrying **carbon dioxide**. Carbon dioxide is bad for your body. Your body must get rid of it. Your heart sends the blood full of carbon dioxide to your **lungs**.

Breathing out pushes carbon dioxide out of your body.

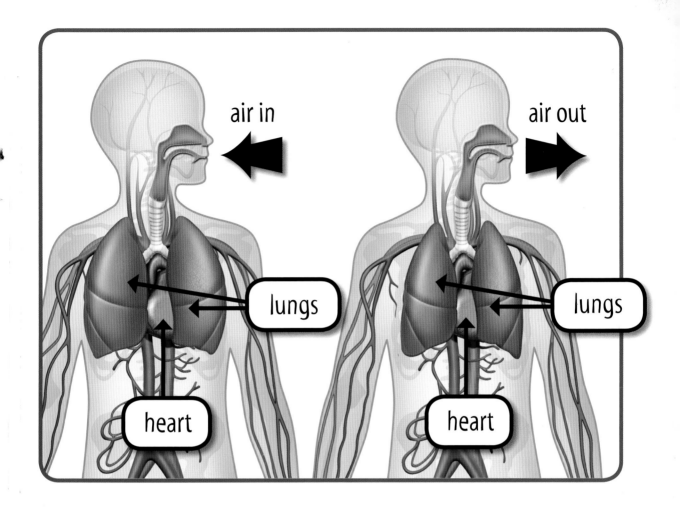

air in

air out

lungs

lungs

heart

heart

Carbon dioxide moves out of your blood and into the air in your lungs. Then when you breathe out, the carbon dioxide moves out of your body. When you breathe in, **oxygen** from the air moves into your blood. The blood is pumped back to the heart, and then around your body again.

The Circulatory System

The circulatory system works to carry blood to every part of your body, from the top of your head to the tips of your fingers and toes.

⇧ **You need blood to keep your body working.**

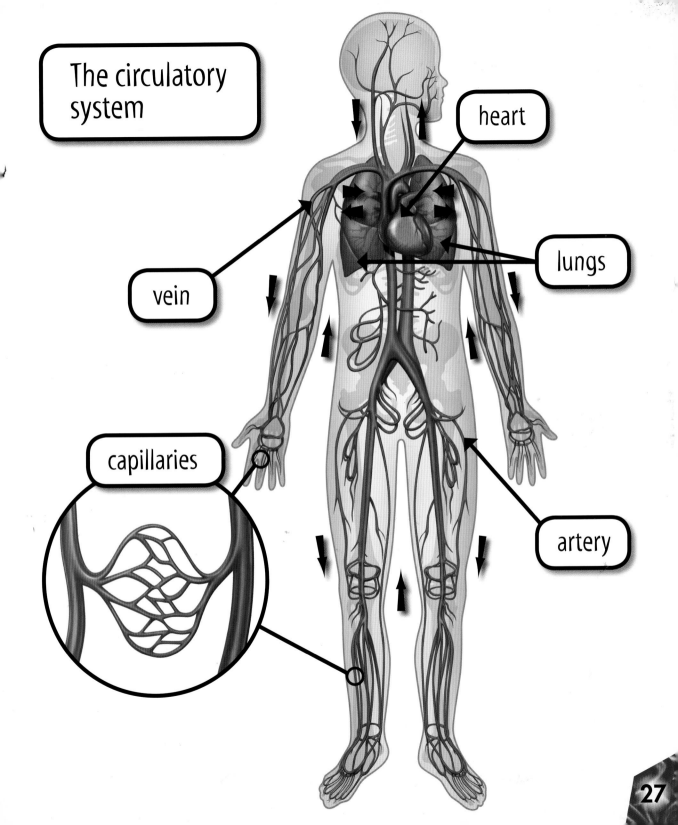

The circulatory system

heart

vein

lungs

capillaries

artery

Why Does My Heart Beat?

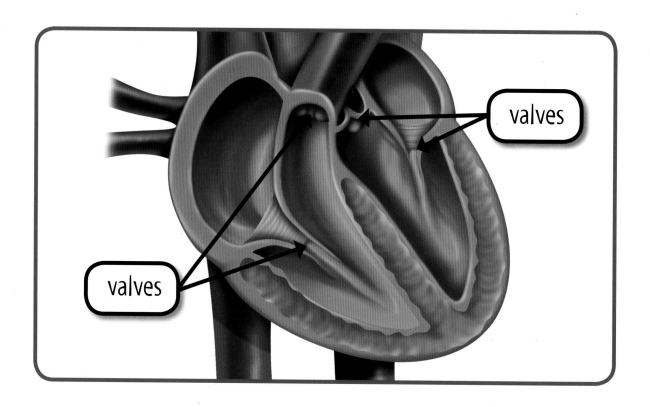

valves

valves

Your **heart** beats to pump blood around your body. The heartbeat sound is made because your heart has different sections with valves between them. The valves are like doors that open and close to let blood in and out. The sound you hear is your valves shutting.

Did You Know?

Your heart is about the size of your fist.

When you are resting, your heart beats about 60 to 80 times a minute.

Red blood **cells** are made in your bones.

Your heart pumps all your blood around your body about 1,000 times each day.

Blood cells are so small that one tiny drop of blood holds millions of blood cells.

29

Glossary

artery   tube that carries blood away from the heart to other parts of the body

blood vessel   tube that carries blood

capillary   tiny tube that links arteries and veins

carbon dioxide   gas that your body needs to get rid of

cell   tiny living part that fits together with other cells to make your body

clot   form a lump

energy   power used to make things happen. Energy can make things grow, change, or move.

glucose   simple sugar that your body uses to get energy

heart   part of the body that pumps blood around

lung   part of the body that is used for breathing air in and out

nutrient   substance your body needs to live and grow

oxygen   gas found in the air that your body uses to produce energy. We need to breathe in oxygen to stay alive.

plasma   clear liquid part of blood

platelet   tiny blood cell that makes your blood thicker to stop bleeding caused by cuts

pulse   movement made by the pumping of your heart. You can feel your pulse in your wrist or on the side of your neck.

vein   tube that carries blood to the heart from other parts of the body

waste   unwanted material. It is often what is left after useful parts have been taken out.

Find Out More

Books to Read

Jen Green. *My Healthy Body: Blood and Heart.* London, UK: Hachette, 2003.

Royston, Angela. *Look After Yourself: Get Some Exercise!.* Chicago: Heinemann Library, 2003.

Thomas, Pat and Lesley Harker. *My Amazing Body: A First Look at Health and Fitness.* London, UK: Hodder Wayland, 2002.

Websites

http://kidshealth.org/kid/body/heart_SW.html
Find out about your heart and how you can keep it healthy by exercising and eating healthy foods.

http://science.nationalgeographic.com/science/ health-and-human-body/human-body
Explore the heart and how it works. Click on "pumping action" to find out how your heartbeat changes when you exercise.

Index